Diet recommendations for hepatic encephalopathy

Please check these recommendations always with a nutrition consultant, therapist, doctor or dietician. The recipes and the list of ingredients are supporting the conventional medical therapy.
The calorie disclosures of fresh ingredients (fruit and vegetables) vary according to quality and time of harvest. The contents were checked by a dietician and a nutrition consultant for the Traditional Chinese Medicine (TCM).

Author:
©2017 Josef Miligui
www.ebns.at

AF236591

Source:
The lists are created from the EBNS database for nutritional counseling. The database is used by dietitians, therapists and doctors for advising the patient / client.

Literature:
The specialist literature and the training documents of the German and Austrian dietary and traditional Chinese medicine serve as a knowledge base. We have used the documents as a basis of knowledge, adapted it to our experience and completed them.
http://di-book.com

Title Photo:
©2008 Erika Weixlbaumer

Production and publishing:
BoD – Books on Demand, Norderstedt
ISBN: 9783752892536

Diet recommendations for DIETETICS - Metabolism - Hepatic encephalopathy

1 Treatment strategy

The challenge of a diet for hepatic encephalopathy is to provide sufficient protein, but largely to dispense with meat and sausage products. These are the main cause for the production of ammonia.
In order to provide enough protein to the patient's body, the loss of meat consumption is compensated above all by dairy products such as plugs or vegetable protein supplements such as soy products and legumes.
The dietary supplementation with special amino acid preparations also represents a possibility.
Both, the control of the protein intake and the sufficient supply of fiber-rich dietary, are component of the diet.
It has been shown that the digestion of dietary fibers helps ammonia to be excreted more over the stool and not to be broken down by the liver in smaller amounts.

2 Avoid

Meat and sausage products.

3 Breakfast

	kkal. per serving
Barley and vegetable soup	281
Barley soup	265
Bean paste piquant sweet	311
Beery dream	273
Broccoli and Parmesan spread on toast bread	148
Bulgur with tomatoes and fresh herbs	205
Chickpeas with Raisins	429
Cottage cheese with steamed fruit	214
Couscous Salad	338
Cous-Cous with date, coco and almondpuree	483
Cream cheese substitute	526
Curry rice with raisins and nuts	275

4 Snack

5 Lunch

6   Afternoon

7   Dinner

8   Any time

9 Recipes

(recommendable) = You can use more.
(little) = You should use less than specified or omit.

9.1 Apricot Oat Balls with Acai powder

Strengthens immune system, little laxative, antioxidativ.
Cooking time approx. 20 min
Calories p. portion: 768
2 portions
Allergens: AHO

Quantity of ingredients:
Oat flakes (whole grain) 1/4 lbs - 4oz / 125g. (yes)
Apricot dried 1/4 lbs - 4oz / 125g. (yes)
Almond 1/4 lbs - 4oz / 100g. (yes)
Honey 2 table spoons / 14g. (yes)
Acai powder 3 teaspoons / 9g. (yes)
Lemon juice 2 table spoons / 9g. (yes)

Cooking instructions:
Lightly chop the sliced almonds in the pan and let them cool. Then pour the apricots in the blender and add lemon juice. Mix all the ingredients together. If the mass is too loose add some honey. Finally, form small balls and roll them in oat flakes.

9.2 Barley and vegetable soup

Supports urination, detoxifying, promotes spleen and liver, reduces blood pressure, strengthens immune system, prevents cancer, reduces radiation damage, promotes digestion, helps to digest fat, harmonizes metabolism.
Cooking time approx. 2 hours
Calories p. portion: 281
3 portions
Allergens: AGL

Quantity of ingredients:
Barley 1 cup / 120g. (yes)
Shiitake, dried 1/8 oz / 4g. (yes)
Onion (shallot) 1 piece / 20g. (yes)
Cumin (Caraway seed) 1 knife tip / 0,5g. (yes)
Sunflower oil 1 table spoon / 10g. (yes)

Water 1 cup / 250g. (yes)
Celery sticks 2 branches / 20g. (yes)
Peas, green 5/8 lbs - 8oz / 250g. (yes)
Tomato 1 piece / 50g. (yes)
Carrot 2 pieces / 150g. (yes)
French beans Handful / 30g. (yes)
Salt 1 pinch / 1g. (yes)
Pepper (ground) 1 pinch / 0,5g. (yes)
Parsley 1 teaspoon / 3g. (yes)
Butter organic 1 teaspoon / 3g. (yes)

Cooking instructions:
Soak the barley in the evening for the next day. Soak the mushrooms separately at the next day. Brown onion and cumin in oil, then boil with water. Add the chopped vegetables, some salt, the barley and the shiitake mushrooms and cook everything to a thick soup. At the end, season with pepper, parsley and a little butter.

9.3 Barley soup

Diuretic, forcing spleen, supports urination, stimulates liver function, antioxidativ, promotes digestion, detoxifying, reduces blood lipids, stimulates, dissolves stagnation.
Cooking time approx. 25 min
Calories p. portion: 265
2 portions
Allergens: A

Quantity of ingredients:
Barley 1 cup / 120g. (yes)
Salt 1 pinch / 1g. (yes)
Ginger fresh 1/2 teaspoon / 1g. (yes)
Olive oil 1 table spoon / 10g. (yes)
Parsley 2 table spoons / 30g. (yes)
Water 1 1/2 cups / 240g. (yes)

Cooking instructions:
Roast the barley in the pan, then grind it to the ground, and boil with water, some salt and ginger to a mash. Before serving add oil and parsley.

Variant: You can add a better taste to the dish if you cook it with prepared vegetable or meat broth.

9.4   Basic recipe for a beef broth (clear)

Strengthens muscles, tendons and bones, reduces blood pressure, strengthens immune system, prevents cancer, reduces radiation damage, stimulates digestion, reduces pain, promotes digestion, diuretic. Rosemary stimulates digestion.
Cooking time approx. 4-8 hours
Calories p. portion: 114
10 portions
Allergens: O

Quantity of ingredients:
Beef soup meat 1,1 lbs / 500g. (little)
Beef meatbones 5/8 oz / 200g. (yes)
Vinegar (Red wine vinegar) 1 dash / 3g. (yes)
Juniper berry 8 pieces / 6g. (yes)
Rosemary 1 pinch / 1g. (yes)
Carrot 3 pieces / 210g. (yes)
Parsnip 2 pieces / 300g. (yes)
Leek 1 piece / 200g. (yes)
Ginger fresh 1/2 teaspoon / 5g. (yes)
Lovage 1 stem / 15g. (yes)
Clove 2 pieces / 2g. (yes)
Pimento 6 pieces / 12g. (yes)
Anise (Common Fennel) 2 pieces / 1g. (yes)
Salt 1 teaspoon / 5g. (yes)
Water 3,3 lbs / 1300g. (yes)

Cooking instructions:
Heat water, a dash of red wine vinegar, some juniper berries, a little rosemary, bones and meat till it boils; add carrot, parsnip, leek, ginger, lovage, clove, allspice, star anise and a little salt; simmer for 4-8 hours then strain. Refrigerate for later use.

9.5   Basic recipe for a chicken broth worming

Strengthens blood, strengthens bone marrow, reduces blood pressure, strengthens immune system, prevents cancer, reduces radiation damage, promotes sweating, dissolves stagnation, good to fight loss of appetite, flatulence.
Cooking time approx. 2-3 hours
Calories p. portion: 90
9 portions
Allergens: L

Quantity of ingredients:
Chicken meat 1/2 piece / 600g. (little)
Carrot 2 pieces / 150g. (yes)
Leek 1 stick / 45g. (yes)
Celery root 1 piece / 500g. (yes)
Ginger fresh 2 slices / 2g. (yes)
Fenugreek (Trigonella foenum-graecum) 1 teaspoon / 2g. (yes)
Juniper berry 1 teaspoon / 3g. (yes)
Bay leaf 3 pieces / 2g. (yes)
Water 4 cup / 900g. (yes)

Cooking instructions:
Remove chicken parts from fat. Place chicken pieces in a saucepan with hot water and heat till it boils briefly, skimming any resulting foam. Add coarsely chopped vegetables and all spices and cook over medium heat for 2 to 3 hours. Strain the finished soup. Throw away vegetables and bones.
Tip: If you want to use the meat as a soup insert, take out after 45 minutes and return only the bones in the soup. Refrigerate for later use.

9.6   Basic recipe for a duck broth

Forcing spleen, strengthens blood, supports urination, reduces blood pressure, strengthens immune system, prevents cancer, reduces radiation damage.
Cooking time approx. 2-3 hours
Calories p. portion: 61
6 portions
Allergens: L

Quantity of ingredients:
Water 2 cup / 450g. (yes)
Duck (heart) 5/8 oz / 200g. ()
Duck (slaughtered) 1/4 lbs - 4oz / 100g. ()
Carrot 2 pieces / 100g. (yes)
Celery root 1/2 piece / 600g. (yes)

Cooking instructions:
Cook duck pieces with vegetables for 2-3 hours. Sift broth through a fine sieve and refrigerate for later use.
The innards can be reused: You cut them finely and leaves them for a few minutes with fresh vegetables in the broth draw. Sprinkle with parsley before serving.

9.7 Basic recipe for a vegetable soup, nutritious

Reduces blood pressure, strengthens immune system, prevents cancer, forcing spleen, dissolves stagnation, promotes weight loss. Good to fight immunodeficiency, high blood pressure, depressions, diabetes, diarrhea, reduces blood lipids.
Cooking time approx. 2-3 hours
Calories p. portion: 48
5 portions
Allergens: L

Quantity of ingredients:
Olive oil 1 table spoon / 4g. (yes)
Onion white 1 piece / 60g. (yes)
Carrot 3 pieces / 200g. (yes)
Parsnip 3/8 lbs - 6oz / 150g. (yes)
Celery root 1 cup / 100g. (yes)
Ginger fresh 1/2 teaspoon / 2g. (yes)
Lemon 1/2 piece / 25g. (yes)
Juniper berry 6 pieces / 6g. (yes)
Thyme dried 1 pinch / 1g. (yes)
Lovage 1 table spoon / 3g. (yes)
Bay leaf 2 leaves / 1g. (yes)
Salt 1 pinch / 1g. (yes)
Water 3 cups / 650g. (yes)

Cooking instructions:
Cut the vegetables into cubes.
Heat oil in hot pot, fry shortly onions and vegetables.
Add cold water, then add ginger, bay leaf and lemon juice.
Season with juniper, thyme and lovage. Cover for 2 - 3 hours on a low heat and simmer.
The used vegetables should be thrown away.
The basic recipe serves as a soup base and to refine vegetables, legumes or cereals.
If you want to eat vegetable soup immediately, add the desired vegetables half an hour before.
Refrigerate for later use.

9.8   Bean paste piquant sweet

Supports urination, lowers cholesterol, prevents arteriosclerosis, antioxidativ. Promotes digestion, helps to digest fat, supports urination, reduces blood pressure.
Cooking time approx. 1 hour
Calories p. portion: 311
1 portions
Allergens: MO

Quantity of ingredients:
Black beans 1 cup / 120g. (yes)
Ginger fresh 1 inch / 3g. (yes)
Boxhorn clover seeds 1/2 teaspoon / 2g. (yes)
Tomato paste 1 table spoon / 10g. (yes)
Olive oil 2 table spoons / 20g. (yes)
Pumpkin seed oil 1 dash / 3g. (yes)
Mustard 1 knife tip / 1g. (yes)
Radish horseradish 1 teaspoon (grated) / 2g. (yes)
Pepper (ground) 1 pinch / 0,5g. (yes)
Garlic 2 cloves / 3g. (yes)
Salt 1 pinch / 1g. (yes)
Sugar molasses 2 table spoons / 20g. (yes)
Lemon peel 1/2 piece / 1g. (yes)

Cooking instructions:
Boil beans (with spices and ginger), drain water and puree. Season with spices.

Refine with sugar beet syrup and lemon peel.

9.9   Beery dream

Good to fight acute or chronic constipation of the intestine. Strengthens immune system, activates cell metabolism.
Cooking time approx. 10 min
Calories p. portion: 274
2 portions
Allergens: G

Quantity of ingredients:
Coconut grated 2 table spoons / 20g. (yes)
Cardamom 1 teaspoon (powder) / 2g. (yes)
Salt 1 pinch / 1g. (yes)
Sheep's milk yoghurt 1 cup / 250g. (recommended)
Berries of the season 5/8 lbs - 8oz / 250g. (yes)
Chocolate 1 rib bitter 70% / 8g. (yes)
Honey 1 table spoon / 10g. (yes)
Amaranth Pops 4 table spoons / 30g. (recommended)

Cooking instructions:
Rub the dark chocolate or chop it roughly with a knife. Wash the
berries, pat dry and put aside some berries. Mix the sheep's milk
yoghurt in a bowl with the chocolate, grated coconut, cardamom powder
and the pinch of salt.
Divide the berries on two bowls and cover with yoghurt. Garnish with
the remaining berries and Amaranth POPS.
If necessary sweeten with honey.

9.10 Bilberry - curd cheese with Acai powder

Good to fight weakness, belching, diabetes, acute or chronic
obstruction of the bowel, skin problems. Laxative, antibacterial effect.
Antioxidant.
Cooking time approx. 10 min
Calories p. portion: 238
2 portions
Allergens: GH

Quantity of ingredients:
Blueberry 5/8 oz / 200g. (yes)
Orange juice 2 table spoons / 10g. (yes)
Maple syrup 1 table spoon / 5g. (yes)
Almond 1 table spoon / 5g. (yes)
Curd cheese 20% 5/8 lbs - 8oz / 250g. (recommended)
Sugar cane sugar 1 table spoon / 9g. (yes)
Acai powder 2 teaspoons / 5g. (yes)
Cinnamon ground 1 pinch / 0,5g. (yes)

Cooking instructions:
Rinse the blueberries in a sieve and pat dry gently. Drizzle with orange
juice and maple syrup and stir in the Acai powder.

Roast the almond sticks in a frying pan until golden brown until they are fragrant and allow to cool on a plate. Dust with a little cinnamon.

Stir quark and sugar until smooth.

Layer alternately the quark with the marinated blueberries in glasses and garnish with the almonds.

9.11 Broccoli and Parmesan spread on toast bread

Good to fight loss of appetite, blood clotting, thyroid function, increase Vitamin B12, strengthen immune system, good to fight belching, diabetes, acute or chronic constipation, dissolves stagnation.
Cooking time approx. 15 min
Calories p. portion: 148
2 portions
Allergens: AG

Quantity of ingredients:
Broccoli 5/8 oz / 200g. (yes)
Curd cheese 20% 3 oz / 80g. (recommended)
Yogurt (natural, 1.5% fat) 1 table spoon / 10g. (recommended)
Parmesan 2 table spoons / 15g. (yes)
Lemon peel 1/2 teaspoon / 1g. (yes)
Basil (fresh) 1 table spoon / 5g. (yes)
Chives 1 table spoon / 5g. (yes)
Salt 1 pinch / 1g. (yes)
Pepper (ground) 1 pinch / 0,3g. (yes)
Toast bread (whole grain) 6 slices / 24g. (yes)

Cooking instructions:
Cook broccoli in a sieve insert over steam for 8 minutes until firm. Finely chop broccoli.
Mix the curd, yoghurt, parmesan and lemon peel well. Mix cheese cream with broccoli, basil and chives. Season the spread with salt and pepper. Serve on the crunchy toasted toast.

9.12 Bulgur with tomatoes and fresh herbs

Promotes digestion, helps to digest fat, supports urination, reduces blood pressure. Stimulates digestion, supports urination.
Cooking time approx. 30 min
Calories p. portion: 205
1 portions
Allergens: A

Quantity of ingredients:
Bulgur (cereals) 1 cup / 120g. (recommended)
Tomato 2 pieces / 70g. (yes)
Rucola 2 table spoons / 16g. (yes)
Pepper powder (hot) 1 pinch / 2g. (yes)
Olive oil 2 table spoons / 20g. (yes)
Pepper (ground) 1 pinch / 0,5g. (yes)
Salt 1 pinch / 1g. (yes)
Basil 4 leaves / 2g. (yes)
Thyme 1 Twig / 3g. (yes)
Lemon juice 1/2 piece / 10g. (yes)

Cooking instructions:
Put cold water in a pot, sprinkle in Bulgur and simmer. Stir in chopped tomatoes, fresh herbs like basil, thyme, arugula, a pinch of rose paprika, lemon juice, a dash of olive oil, a little ground pepper, some salt.

Variant: add some mozzarella.

Recommendation: ideal morning meal in summer; also suitable as evening meal, especially for sleep disorders.

9.13 Chickpeas with Raisins

Reduces blood pressure, strengthens immune system. Relaxes breast pressure, moisturizer dry skin, helps to fight incontinence. Strengthens spleen and stomach, strengthens the muscles.
Cooking time approx. 45 min
Calories p. portion: 429
2 portions
Allergens: EGO

Quantity of ingredients:
Chickpeas 1 cup / 120g. (recommended)
Hijiki 1 table spoon / 7g. (yes)
Salt 1 pinch / 0,5g. (yes)
Sunflower oil 1 table spoon / 10g. (yes)
Carrot 2 pieces / 160g. (yes)
Raisins 2 table spoons / 18g. (yes)
Ginger fresh 1/2 teaspoon / 2g. (yes)
Cumin (Caraway seed) 1 pinch / 0,2g. (yes)
Lemon juice 1 dash / 1g. (yes)
Sour cream 15% fat 1 table spoon / 8g. (little)
Curcuma 1 pinch / 0,2g. (yes)
Soybean milk 1 dash / 1g. (recommended)
Coriander 1 pinch / 0,2g. (yes)
Soy sauce 1 dash / 1g. (yes)
Rice round grain 1/2 cup / 60g. (yes)
Water 3 cups / 250g. (yes)
Salt 1 pinch / 1g. (yes)

Cooking instructions:
Preparation:
Soak chickpeas in cold water for several hours or overnight.

After that:
Pour soaking water away; put the chickpeas in cold water; Add 1 tbsp
Hijiki and cook the chickpeas bite-proof;
Add salt at the end of the cooking time.

Separately:
In a hot pan, fry oil, chopped carrots (more than chickpeas), raisins,
grated ginger, plenty of cumin and salt until the carrots are half cooked;
add the chickpeas and sea algae; Add lemon juice, a little sour cream,
turmeric, soy or rice milk; a pinch of cilantro, add some soy sauce; Let it
soak for a few minutes over low heat until the carrots are cooked.

Put the round grain rice with the water, salt and cook for about 20
minutes.

9.14 Cottage cheese with steamed fruit

Good to fight loss of appetite, promotes digestion, supports urination.
Cooking time approx. 20 min
Calories p. portion: 214
2 portions
Allergens: G

Quantity of ingredients:
Cottage cheese 3/4 lbs / 300g. (recommended)
Apple (sour) 1 piece / 100g. (yes)
Pear 1 piece / 100g. (yes)

Cooking instructions:
Wash apples and pears well, do not peel, and chop small. In a pot with steam filter, boil them al dente, remove and allow to cool down.
Serve the cheese, spread the fruit on it.

9.15 Couscous Salad

prevents cancer, forcing spleen, promotes digestion, stimulates liver function, reduces blood pressure, strengthens immune system, reduces radiation damage, diuretic.
Cooking time approx. 25 min
Calories p. portion: 338
3 portions
Allergens: A

Quantity of ingredients:
Water 1 cup / 100g. (yes)
Olive oil 1 table spoon / 15g. (yes)
Couscous 5/8 oz / 200g. (yes)
Lemon juice 2 table spoons / 30g. (yes)
Lemon peel 1 teaspoon / 2g. (yes)
Tomato 2 pieces / 80g. (yes)
Cucumber 1/4 lbs - 4oz / 100g. (yes)
Carrot 1/4 lbs - 4oz / 100g. (yes)
Parsley 1 Bunch / 100g. (yes)
Chives 1 Bunch / 100g. (yes)
Peppermint 3 twigs / 30g. (yes)

Cooking instructions:
Boil in a small saucepan 250 ml. water with salt and 1 tablespoon olive oil. Add the couscous, take the stove in the front and let it swell covered

for 5 minutes. Put the couscous back on the stove and let it simmer for about 2 minutes with gentle stirring. If necessary, add 1 - 3 tbsp of hot water.
Mix the couscous with lemon juice, chopped lemon peel and 1 tbsp oil, season with salt and pepper and leave to set.
Add couscous with tomatoes, cucumber, parsley (all diced), carrots (grated), chives and mint (finely chopped).
Season the couscous salad with lemon juice, salt and pepper.

9.16 Cous-Cous with date, coco and almondpuree

Stops diarrhea, promotes digestion, appetizing, relieves diarrhea.
Cooking time approx. 10 min
Calories p. portion: 484
3 portions
Allergens: AHO

Quantity of ingredients:
Couscous 1 1/2 cups / 240g. (yes)
Water 4 cups / 400g. (yes)
Dates dried 6 pieces / 20g. (yes)
Coconut flakes 2 table spoons / 30g. (yes)
Almond puree 2 table spoons / 20g. (yes)
Olive oil 2 teaspoons / 20g. (yes)
Apple (sweet) 1 piece grated / 120g. (yes)
Vanilla 1 knife tip / 0,2g. (yes)

Cooking instructions:
Put couscous and olive oil in a large bowl and pour boiling water over them. Let it swell for 10 minutes. Crush dates and grate apple. Loosen up cous-cous with a fork. Mix in dates, coconut flakes, apple and almond paste.
Sweet to taste. Spices and flavors: vanilla, little chili

Winter variation: pear,
Summer variation: apricot, nectarine

9.17 Cream cheese substitute

Good to fight lactose intolerance. Strengthens body energy, promotes digestion, promotes weight loss. Good to fight immunodeficiency, loss of appetite, arteriosclerosis, flatulence, bladder weakness, anemia, high blood pressure, depressions, diabetes, diarrhea.
Cooking time approx. 20 min
Calories p. portion: 526
2 portions
Allergens: AE

Quantity of ingredients:
Soybean milk 4 cup / 300g. (recommended)
Lemon 1 piece / 50g. (yes)
Herbs various 2 table spoons / 6g. (yes)
Whole grain bread 6 slices / 300g. (yes)

Cooking instructions:
Heat the soy milk in a saucepan till it boils, stirring occasionally (gets burn easily!), Then allow to cool.
Squeeze out the lemon and stir gently under the cooled soy milk (approx. 80°C/176°F), let it approx. 20 min. rest or clot.
Pour chopped soy milk through a strainer lined with a dishcloth, allow liquid to drain and then squeeze out remaining liquid with the dishcloth.
Refine to taste with fresh herbs.
Serve with wholemeal bread.

9.18 Curry rice with raisins and nuts

Stops diarrhea, promotes digestion, appetizing, harmonizes the stomach, improves blood circulation, improves medication effect, stimulates appetite, detoxifies the skin, stimulates nerves, frees breathing, increases body temperature, promotes perspiration.
Cooking time approx. 30 min
Calories p. portion: 275
4 portions
Allergens: HO

Quantity of ingredients:
Sunflower oil 1 table spoon / 15g. (yes)
Onion white 1 piece / 50g. (yes)
Curry 1/2 teaspoon / 2g. (yes)
Rice wild (nature rice) 1 cup / 120g. (yes)
Salt 1 pinch / 1g. (yes)

White wine 1/2 cup / 125g. (yes)
Lemon Alternatively for white wine / g. (yes)
Peppers powder 1 pinch / 1g. (yes)
Apple (sweet) 2 pieces / 300g. (yes)
Raisins 2 table spoons / 25g. (yes)
Walnuts 2 table spoons / 25g. (yes)
Water 6 cups / 500g. (yes)

Cooking instructions:
Heat oil in a pot; fry chopped onions until glassy; add the curry and let it foam for a short time; then fry the raw rice for a few minutes over a gentle heat, stirring constantly; Salt, a dash of white wine or lemon juice, rose paprika, sweet apples chopped, raisins, chopped, roasted nuts added; pour hot water on it until well covered; simmer until the rice is cooked.

Goes well with: carrot and fennel vegetables, legumes with boiled vegetables, sliced poultry with ginger and mushrooms.

9.19 Grilled tomatoes with cheese filling

Promotes digestion, helps to digest fat, supports urination, reduces blood pressure, stimulates digestion.
Cooking time approx. 30 min
Calories p. portion: 470
2 portions
Allergens: ACG

Quantity of ingredients:
Tomato 8 pieces / 200g. (yes)
Feta cheese 0,2 lbs / 75g. (recommended)
Fresh cheese 0,2 lbs / 75g. (yes)
Chicken egg 1 piece / 60g. (little)
Olive oil 1 table spoon / 12g. (yes)
Basil (fresh) 1 table spoon / 6g. (yes)
Salt 1 pinch / 1g. (yes)
Pepper (ground) 1 pinch / 0,5g. (yes)
Olives 1 oz / 30g. (yes)
Rucola 1/4 lbs / 100g. (yes)
White bread (wheat bread) 4 slices / 80g. (yes)

Cooking instructions:
Hollow out tomatoes generously. Put in a casserole dish.
Mix cheese, olive oil, egg, chopped basil and flour. Season with salt and pepper and fill in the tomatoes.
Bake in the preheated oven at 210 degrees on the middle rail for 15 minutes, then switch on the oven grill and grill for a further 3 minutes (without circulating air).
Stone the olives and chop and sprinkle on the tomatoes.
Garnish tomatoes with rocket and serve with white bread.

9.20 Hummus (Chickpeas mash)

Relaxes breast pressure, moisturizer dry skin, helps to fight incontinence, antioxidativ. Stimulates liver function, detoxifying, stimulates the immune system, dissolves stagnation.
Cooking time approx. 2 hours
Calories p. portion: 542
2 portions
Allergens: N

Quantity of ingredients:
Chickpeas 1 1/2 cups / 240g. (recommended)
Wakame 1 teaspoon (grated) / 2g. (yes)
Ginger fresh 1/4 teaspoon / 1g. (yes)
Rosemary 1 pinch / 0,5g. (yes)
Sesame paste (Tahini) 1 table spoon / 10g. (yes)
Olive oil 2 table spoons / 20g. (yes)
Lemon juice 1 dash / 2g. (yes)
Water upon need / g. (yes)
Garlic 1 clove (scraped) / 2g. (yes)
Parsley 1 teaspoon (chopped) / 2g. (yes)
Peppers 1 pinch / 0,2g. (yes)
Curcuma 1 pinch / 0,2g. (yes)
Coriander 1 pinch / 0,2g. (yes)
Cardamom 1 pinch / 0,2g. (yes)
Pepper (ground) 1 pinch / 0,2g. (yes)
Salt (herbal) 1/2 teaspoon / 2g. (yes)

Cooking instructions:
Soak chickpeas overnight or for at least 6 hours, pour off soaking water, boil in fresh water for about 1 to 1 ½ hours with a little seaweed and ginger, allow to cool.
Seasoning with a few splashes of lemon juice and parsley.

Add the pepper, garlic cut into small pieces or pressed, more or less coriander and cardamom powder, little chili powder as desired, tahin and olive oil.

Puree all ingredients together. Depending on the consistency, add water. It should be a smooth paste.
Spread on cereal, crackers or toasted bread or enjoy with salad.

9.21 Italian Vegetable and Bean Soup

Promotes digestion, helps to digest fat, supports urination, reduces blood pressure. Stimulates blood production and metabolism, reduces fat, reduces blood pressure, strengthens immune system.
Cooking time approx. 1 hour
Calories p. portion: 204
4 portions
Allergens: L

Quantity of ingredients:
Butter beans white 5/8 oz / 200g. (yes)
Onion (shallot) 1 piece / 20g. (yes)
Carrot 1 piece / 70g. (yes)
Olive oil 2 table spoons / 20g. (yes)
Tomato 2 pieces / 80g. (yes)
Celery root 1/4 lbs / 100g. (yes)
White cabbage 0,2 lbs / 70g. (yes)
Endive salad 1/8 lbs - 2oz / 50g. (yes)
Salt 1 pinch / 1g. (yes)
Pepper (ground) 1 pinch / 0,2g. (yes)
Water 2 cup / 450g. (yes)

Cooking instructions:
Soak beans and cook for 1/2 hour.
Fry onions, carrots and celery in frying oil.
Add tomatoes and water and simmer for 30 minutes.
Cut white cabbage into strips. Add the cabbage and endive salad and the boiled beans, and season with salt,
pepper and olive oil.

9.22 Lasagne with tofu cream

Harmonizes spleen and stomach, reduces Flatulence, protects the digestive system. Good to fight lack of appetite, flatulence, inflammatory bowel disease, stomach ulcers, rheumatism, heartburn, twelffinger intestinal ulcers.
Cooking time approx. 45 min
Calories p. portion: 301
4 portions
Allergens: ACEG

Quantity of ingredients:
Soy Tofu 7/8 lbs / 400g. (recommended)
Chicken egg 2 pieces / 100g. (little)
Onion white 2 pieces / 120g. (yes)
Tomato 1/4 lbs - 4oz / 100g. (yes)
Oregano dried 1 pinch / 1g. (yes)
Marjoram 1 pinch / 1g. (yes)
Peppers powder 1 pinch / 1g. (yes)
Salt 1 pinch / 1g. (yes)
Noodles (wheat, lasagne) with egg 3/8 lbs - 6oz / 150g. (yes)
Edam cheese 1/8 lbs - 2oz / 50g. (yes)

Cooking instructions:
Tofu cream: Mix tofu with eggs, onions, small tomatoes, oregano, marjoram, peppers and some sea salt put into a smooth mass using a kitchen machine with a knife or a blender.

Lasagne: Place 1/5 of the tofu cream in a casserole dish (25x15cm), cover with 3 lasagna leaves, repeat this process twice, and then finish the last fifth of the tofu cream over the pastry plates. Sprinkle with a little grated
Edam and bake in the oven at 175°C/347°F for about 1/2 hour.

9.23 Lettuce with fresh cheese

The bitter substances have diuretic effect and promote the blood circulation in the digestive area. Mustard improves thyroid function, relieves rheumatism symptoms.
Cooking time approx. 5 min
Calories p. portion: 802
1 portions
Allergens: AFM

Quantity of ingredients:
Leaf salads (bitter) 2 portions / 60g. (yes)
Fresh cheese from soya 3/8 lbs - 6oz / 150g. (recommended)
Mustard 1 knife tip / 1g. (yes)
Lemon juice 1 dash / 3g. (yes)
Salt 1 pinch / 1g. (yes)
Pepper (ground) 1 pinch / 0,5g. (yes)
Herbs various 2 teaspoons / 4g. (yes)
Black caraway 1 pinch / 1g. (yes)
Whole grain bread 2 slices / 40g. (yes)

Cooking instructions:
Wash lettuce and finely pluck.
Mix 150 ml cream cheese, splashes of mustard, splashes of lemon
juice, 1 clove of garlic, chopped fresh herbs, pinch of pepper and
crushed black cumin and pour over. Serve with wholemeal bread.

9.24 Mung bean stew

Relieves excessive thirst, supports urination, reduces blood lipids,
relieves allergies. Strengthens spleen and stomach, strengthens the
muscles. Lowers cholesterol, antiparasitic. Stimulates liver function,
detoxifying.
Cooking time approx. 2 hours
Calories p. portion: 665
2 portions
Allergens:

Quantity of ingredients:
Mung bean 5/8 lbs - 8oz - 500g / 300g. (recommended)
Sunflower oil 2 table spoons / 30g. (yes)
Amaranth 1/2 teaspoon / 2g. (recommended)
Fennel seeds ground 1/2 teaspoon / 2g. (yes)
Cumin (Caraway seed) 1/2 teaspoon / 2g. (yes)
Coriander 1/2 teaspoon / 2g. (yes)
Rice round grain 1/2 cup / 60g. (yes)
Water 3 cups / 300g. (yes)
Ginger fresh 1 inch / 3g. (yes)
Kombu seaweed (Saccharina japonica) 1 inch / 2g. (yes)
Salt 1 pinch / 0,5g. (yes)
Parsley 1 table spoon / 3g. (yes)

Cooking instructions:
Soak mung beans overnight.
Heat sunflower oil in a hot pot. Stir in the amaranth, fennel seeds, cumin and coriander and fry briefly.
admit basmati rice, some ginger and mung beans and roast briefly.
Pour water and heat till it boils.
Add a piece of kombu alga and salt.
Simmer for 1-1/2 hours.
Garnish with parsley or coriander.

9.25 Noodle casserole with plugs and peaches

Relieves fatigue, relaxes, good to fight belching, acute or chronic obstruction of the bowel, flatulence, heartburn. Calms nerves and stomach, strengthens the defense, good to fight fungi infections.
Cooking time approx. 1 hour
Calories p. portion: 442
4 portions
Allergens: ACGO

Quantity of ingredients:
Peaches 1,1 lbs / 500g. (yes)
Noodles (wheat, ribbon noodles) with egg 5/8 oz / 200g. (yes)
Chicken egg 2 pieces / 120g. (little)
Sugar - icing sugar 1/8 lbs - 2oz / 40g. (yes)
Vanilla sugar natural 3 package / 3g. (yes)
Lemon peel 1/2 piece / 2g. (yes)
Cinnamon ground 1/4 teaspoon / 1g. (yes)
Curd cheese 20% 5/8 lbs - 8oz / 250g. (recommended)
Butter organic 2 teaspoons / 8g. (yes)
Strawberry jam 4 table spoons / 50g. (yes)

Cooking instructions:
Preheat oven to 180°C/356°F.
Put Peaches briefly in boiling water, drain and peel off the skin. Cut peaches into small slices.
Cook noodles in plenty of salted water until firm, drain, chill off cold and drain.
Separate eggs. Stir egg yolks with icing sugar, vanilla sugar, grated lemon zest and cinnamon until fluffy with the whisk. Stir in the curd cheese. Add the noodles.
Beat the egg whites into firm snow and carefully lift them under the pasta.

Spread a baking dish thinly with butter. Alternating pate noodle mixture and peach slices into the form layers. Finish with the pasta mixture. Sprinkle the casserole with butter flakes and bake in a preheated oven for 3o minutes.
Serve portion by portion with a tablespoon of jam.

9.26 Noodles with vegetable and tomato sauce

Protects the digestive system. Detoxifying, Good to fight loss of appetite, flatulence, inflammatory bowel disease, obesity, gout, stomach ulcers, stomach cramps, rheumatism, heartburn, twelffinger intestinal ulcers, promotes digestion, helps to digest fat.
Cooking time approx. 45 min
Calories p. portion: 562
2 portions
Allergens: ACG

Quantity of ingredients:
Tomato 1/4 lbs - 4oz / 125g. (yes)
Carrot 1 piece / 80g. (yes)
Zucchini 1 piece / 80g. (yes)
Olive oil 1 table spoon / 15g. (yes)
Onion (shallot) 1 piece / 20g. (yes)
Oregano dried 1 pinch / 1g. (yes)
Salt 1 pinch / 1g. (yes)
Pepper (ground) 1 pinch / 0,2g. (yes)
Noodles (wheat) with egg 5/8 oz / 200g. (yes)
Olive oil 1 table spoon / 10g. (yes)
Créme fraiche cheese 2 table spoons / 30g. (yes)

Cooking instructions:
Boil the tomatoes with a little water, drain and collect the juice, cut the tomatoes into pieces.
Roughly grate zucchini and carrot. Heat olive oil in a pot. Steam shallots very soft. Add tomatoes, season with oregano, salt and pepper. Simmer tomatoes to a thick sauce.
Bring plenty of salted water to boil, cook the wholegrain noodles until firm.
In the cooking time of the pasta, heat in a pan olive oil. Fry the carrots while stirring, lightly salt. Add zucchini, sauté briefly while stirring. The vegetables should be soft with a bite.
Drain pasta, mix with créme fraiche, season with salt and pepper.
Garnish with the tomato sauce.

9.27 Pancakes with spinach and parmesan

Promotes bowel movement, improves blood circulation, forcing spleen and bowel, strengthens immune system, good to fight loss of appetite, flatulence, high blood pressure, depressions, diabetes, constipation, inflammatory bowel disease
Cooking time approx. 25 min
Calories p. portion: 330
6 portions
Allergens: ACGL

Quantity of ingredients:
Wholemeal flour 1/4 lbs - 4oz / 100g. (yes)
Wheat flour 1/4 lbs - 4oz / 100g. (yes)
Chicken egg 4 pieces / 200g. (little)
Cow's milk (whole milk 3.5% fat) 1 1/2 cups / 400g. (yes)
Salt 1 pinch / 1g. (yes)
Sunflower oil 1 table spoon / 15g. (yes)
Olive oil 1 table spoon / 15g. (yes)
Onion white 1 piece / 50g. (yes)
Parsley 1/2 bunch / 80g. (yes)
Basic recipe for a vegetable soup (nutritious) 1/2 cup / 150g. (yes)
Basil (fresh) 1/4 teaspoon / 1g. (yes)
Nutmeg 1 pinch / 0,3g. (yes)
Créme fraiche cheese 2 table spoons / 45g. (yes)
Spinach 1,3 lbs / 600g. (yes)
Salt 1 pinch / 1g. (yes)
Pepper (ground) 1 pinch / 0,1g. (yes)
Parmesan 1/8 lbs - 2oz / 60g. (yes)

Cooking instructions:
Stir flour, eggs and milk and a pinch of salt with the whisk until smooth. From the dough, fry pancakes crispy brown on both sides.

Heat oil in a small saucepan. Fry the finely chopped onion until tender. Stir in chopped parsley, sauté briefly. Add the vegetable broth according to the basic recipe, season with basil and nutmeg. Cover and simmer for 15 minutes, add crème fraiche and finely puree.
Cook the washed, drizzled spinach with a little salt in a closed pan over a moderate heat in 3 minutes, drain in a sieve and cut into small pieces. Add the spinach to the sauce, heat briefly. Add parmesan in the mix.
Fill the pancakes with the cream spinach.

9.28 Pea dish

Supports urination, calms nerves and stomach, soothes embryo during pregnancy. Strengthens gastrointestinal function, expands blood vessels, prevents cancer, prevents diseases (in the elderly).
Cooking time approx. 1-2 hours
Calories p. portion: 406
1 portions
Allergens: CE

Quantity of ingredients:
Peas 3/8 lbs - 6oz (dried) / 150g. (yes)
Lemon 1 piece / 40g. (yes)
Juniper berry 6 pieces / 2g. (yes)
Sunflower oil 1 teaspoon / 3g. (yes)
Pepper white (ground) 1 pinch / 0,3g. (yes)
Bay leaf 3 leaves / 2g. (yes)
Onion white 1 piece / 50g. (yes)
Thyme 1 teaspoon / 2g. (yes)
Ginger fresh 1/2 teaspoon / 1g. (yes)
Chicken egg 1 piece / 60g. (little)
Wakame 1 inch / 2g. (yes)
Salt 1 pinch / 1g. (yes)
Soy sauce per taste / 2g. (yes)

Cooking instructions:
Soak dried peas in plenty of cold water for several hours or overnight. Pour away soaking water and wash peas thoroughly.

Place the peas with about 1 1/2 l of cold water and heat till it boils; cook without lid for 5 minutes; scoop up the foam that forms; only then add the following ingredients: a slice of lemon, juniper berries, oil, peppercorns, bay leaves, chopped onion, dried thyme, chopped ginger, simmer about 2 strips of wakame or 1 tbsp Hijiki with lid closed for 1 - 2 hours; After 1 hour, try if the peas are already soft, because the cooking time changes with the soaking time and the age of aging; when the peas are cooked, remove the lemon slice, juniper berries and peppercorns; with salt, soy sauce, lemon juice to taste.

Note: The dish can be refrigerated for 3-4 days and heated in portions.

Serve with: crispy vegetables, rice or millet steamed in water.

9.29 Pine nuts porridge

Strengthens metabolism, strengthens muscles.
Cooking time approx. 5 min
Calories p. portion: 235
1 portions
Allergens:

Quantity of ingredients:
Pine nuts 2 table spoons / 35g. (yes)

Cooking instructions:
Available in good health food stores.

9.30 Plum Cake

Cancer preventive effect, dehydrates the body, stimulates digestion and
binds fats in the intestine, good to fight loss of appetite, flatulence,
inflammatory bowel disease, obesity, gout, stomach ulcers, stomach
cramps, rheumatism, heartburn. Relieves pain, detoxifying, bactericide.
Cooking time approx. 1 hour
Calories p. portion: 502
6 portions
Allergens: AG

Quantity of ingredients:
Curd cheese 20% 5/8 oz / 200g. (recommended)
Wheat flour 7/8 lbs / 400g. (yes)
Cow's milk (whole milk 3.5% fat) 6 table spoons / 70g. (yes)
Rapeseed oil 6 table spoons / 70g. (yes)
Honey 8 table spoons / 100g. (yes)
Baking powder 1 package / 3g. (yes)
Salt 1 pinch / 1g. (yes)
Cinnamon ground 1 teaspoon / 3g. (yes)
Plums 2,2 lbs / 1000g. (yes)

Cooking instructions:
Mix the flour, curd cheese, milk, oil, honey, salt and baking powder into
a smooth dough. Keep the dough cool for 15 minutes to cool.
Lay out baking paper on a baking sheet and press the dough out to a
bottom.
Now spread the plums evenly.
Sprinkle the cake with the cinnamon and bake for about 40 minutes at
190 ° C/374 °F.

9.31 Potato bags with wild herbs and tomato sauce

Promotes spleen, reduces inflammation, improves digestion, good to fight loss of appetite, flatulence, inflammatory bowel disease, stimulates liver function, promotes urination, dissolves stagnation, detoxifies, supporting prostate disorders.
Cooking time approx. 45 min
Calories p. portion: 418
5 portions
Allergens: ACG

Quantity of ingredients:
Olive oil 1 table spoon / 10g. (yes)
Onion white 1 piece / 50g. (yes)
Garlic 1 piece / 2g. (yes)
Tomato puree 7/8 lbs / 400g. (yes)
Salt 1 pinch / 1g. (yes)
Pepper (ground) 1 pinch / 0,5g. (yes)
Cream, sweet 30% 1 table spoon / 10g. (yes)
Potato 1,4 lbs / 650g. (yes)
Wheat flour 5/8 oz / 200g. (yes)
Chicken egg 1 piece / 60g. (little)
Salt 1 pinch / 1g. (yes)
Pepper (ground) 1 pinch / 0,5g. (yes)
Nutmeg 1 pinch / 0,2g. (yes)
Nettles 1/8 lbs - 2oz / 50g. (yes)
Dandelion (young plants) 1 oz / 30g. (yes)
Yarrow 1 oz / 30g. (yes)
Chervil dried 1/2 oz / 10g. (yes)
Ribworttea 1/2 oz / 10g. (yes)
Parsley 1/8 lbs - 2oz / 50g. (yes)
Olive oil 1 table spoon / 10g. (yes)
Garlic 1 piece / 2g. (yes)
Curd cheese 20% 4 table spoons / 40g. (recommended)
Mayonnaise 50% 1 table spoon / 10g. (yes)
Salt (herbal) 1/2 teaspoon / 2g. (yes)
Black caraway 1 pinch / 1g. (yes)
Pepper (ground) 1 pinch / 0,5g. (yes)
Emmental cheese 1/4 lbs / 100g. (yes)

Cooking instructions:
Tomato sauce:
Heat oil. Roast diced onion briefly with crushed garlic. Add the tomato puree and let it thicken for 2 minutes while stirring, season with salt and pepper and add the cream and place in a fireproof mold.

Potato Batter:
Cook the boiled potato, drain, peel and squeeze. Mix in a bowl with flour, Parmesan, egg and spices. Roll out the dough on a lightly floured work surface and cut into 5 cm squares.

Herb Stuffing:
Chop the herbs and mix with oil, garlic, curd cheese, mayonnaise, herb salt, crushed black cumin and pepper to a creamy mass.

Put on the pastry with a spoon in the middle. Fold into a triangle, press on the edge and let the pockets soak in plenty of salted water until they float up. Add to the tomatoes, sprinkle with the grated cheese and bake in the oven until golden brown.

9.32 Potato cream with herbs and fresh cheese

Good to fight loss of appetite, constipation, bloating and nausea.
Improves digestion, supports urination, prevents cancer, forcing spleen, dissolves stagnation, relaxing and reassuring.
Cooking time approx. 25 min
Calories p. portion: 217
2 portions
Allergens: G

Quantity of ingredients:
Potato (mealy) 5/8 lbs - 8oz / 250g. (yes)
Fresh cheese 3 oz / 80g. (yes)
Yogurt (natural, 1.5% fat) 2 table spoons / 45g. (recommended)
Chives 1/2 bunch / 50g. (yes)
Basil (fresh) 1 teaspoon / 4g. (yes)
Parsley 1 teaspoon / 4g. (yes)
Dill 1/2 teaspoon / 2g. (yes)
Salt 1 pinch / 1g. (yes)
Black caraway 1 pinch / 0,5g. (yes)
Pepper (ground) 1 pinch / 0,5g. (yes)

Cooking instructions:
Softly steam the potatoes in the pan, peel them and press through the potato press.
Mix cream cheese, yoghurt and herbs under the potatoes, season with salt, crushed black cumin and pepper.

9.33 Potatoes with curd cheese sauce

Improves digestion, supports urination, lowers cholesterol. Good to fight weakness, belching, diabetes, acute or chronic obstruction of the bowel, skin problems. Good to fight Bloating, cramping in gastrointestinal complaints.
Cooking time approx. 45 min
Calories p. portion: 414
6 portions
Allergens: G

Quantity of ingredients:
Potato 2,2 lbs / 1000g. (yes)
Curd cheese 20% 1,1 lbs / 500g. (recommended)
Cream, sweet 30% 5/8 oz / 200g. (yes)
Edam cheese 3 oz / 80g. (yes)
Dill 1 Bunch / 100g. (yes)
Corn germ oil 1 teaspoon / 3g. (yes)
Pepper (ground) 1 pinch / 0,2g. (yes)
Salt 1/2 teaspoon / 1g. (yes)
Sunflower seeds 1/8 lbs - 2oz / 40g. (recommended)

Cooking instructions:
Wash the potatoes and cook in plenty of water for about 20 minutes. Stir the creamy cheese with the cream and cottage cheese. Wash the sprouts, finely chop. Stir in with the chopped dill. (For the baby, mix 150 g. of pot with the oil.) Mix the rest with pepper, salt and the sunflower seeds. Peel the potatoes, arrange (for the baby 200 g.)
with the pot.

9.34 Potatoes with wild garlic-curd cheese

Improves digestion, regenerates skin, supports urination, lowers cholesterol. Helps to fight stomach pressure, belching, diabetes, acute or chronic constipation of the intestine. Improves the flow characteristics of the blood.
Cooking time approx. 20 min
Calories p. portion: 254
2 portions
Allergens: G

Quantity of ingredients:
Potato 3/4 lbs / 300g. (yes)
Salt 1 pinch / 0,1g. (yes)
Wild garlic (garlic spinach) 2 handful / 30g. (yes)
Curd cheese 20% 5/8 lbs - 8oz / 250g. (recommended)
Yogurt (natural, 1.5% fat) 2 table spoons / 20g. (recommended)
Salt 1 pinch / 1g. (yes)

Cooking instructions:
Cook potatoes in salted water and peel.
Wash he wild garlic leaves and carefully dried and cut into fine strips.
Mix the cottage cheese, yogurt and salt and
mix in the chopped wild garlic pieces. Serve with the potatoes.
In the season in which no wild garlic grows the wild garlic pesto can be used.

9.35 Pumpkin dumplings with parmesan and parsley sauce

Protects the digestive system. Good to fight loss of appetite, flatulence, calms nerves and stomach, helps to digest fat, reduces blood pressure, stimulates liver function, dissolves stagnation.
Cooking time approx. 30 min
Calories p. portion: 432
2 portions
Allergens: ACG

Quantity of ingredients:
Hokkaido pumpkin 1/4 lbs - 4oz / 100g. (yes)
Chicken egg 2 pieces / 120g. (little)
Wheat flour 1/2-1/3 cup / 120g. (yes)
Salt 1 pinch / 1g. (yes)

Pepper (ground) 1 pinch / 0,5g. (yes)
Nutmeg 1 pinch / 0,2g. (yes)
Lemon peel 1/2 teaspoon / 2g. (yes)
Parmesan 2 table spoons / 20g. (yes)
Onion (spring onion) 2 pieces / 40g. (yes)
Tomato 1/4 lbs - 4oz / 100g. (yes)
Parsley 1/4 Bunch / 15g. (yes)
Salt 1 pinch / 1g. (yes)
Olive oil 1 table spoon / 10g. (yes)
Parmesan 1 table spoon / 7g. (yes)

Cooking instructions:
Peel the pumpkin with a sharp knife, remove the seeds and cut the pulp
into large cubes. Wrap pumpkin in aluminum foil, bake in preheated
oven at 200°C/392°F for 20 minutes. Pour off any spilled pumpkin juice.
Finely crush the pumpkin with the fork. Stir pumpkin and egg until
smooth. Stir in so much flour until a dough is formed, from which
dumplings can be cut off. Season the mixture with lemon zest, salt,
pepper and nutmeg.
Cut off small dumplings with a teaspoon. Leave pumpkin dumplings in
boiling salted water for approx. 7 minutes.

Finely chop the parsley and mix with the olive oil and salt.

Arrange pumpkin dumplings in portions with the parsley sauce.
Parmesan to hand.

9.36 Pumpkin dumplings with tomato and parsley sauce

Protects the digestive system. Good to fight loss of appetite, flatulence,
calms nerves and stomach, helps to digest fat, reduces blood pressure,
stimulates liver function, dissolves stagnation.
Cooking time approx. 30 min
Calories p. portion: 380
2 portions
Allergens: ACG

Quantity of ingredients:
Hokkaido pumpkin 1/4 lbs - 4oz / 100g. (yes)
Chicken egg 2 pieces / 120g. (little)
Wheat flour 1/2-1/3 cup / 120g. (yes)
Salt 1 pinch / 1g. (yes)

Pepper (ground) 1 pinch / 0,5g. (yes)
Nutmeg 1 pinch / 0,2g. (yes)
Lemon peel 1/2 teaspoon / 2g. (yes)
Parmesan 2 table spoons / 20g. (yes)
Onion (spring onion) 2 pieces / 40g. (yes)
Tomato 1/4 lbs - 4oz / 100g. (yes)
Parsley 1/2 bunch / 50g. (yes)
Salt 1 pinch / 1g. (yes)

Cooking instructions:
Peel the pumpkin with a sharp knife, remove the seeds and cut the pulp
into large cubes. Wrap pumpkin in aluminum foil, bake in preheated
oven at 200°C/392°F for 20 minutes. Pour off any spilled pumpkin juice.
Finely crush the pumpkin with the fork. Stir pumpkin and egg until
smooth. Stir in so much flour until a dough is formed, from which
dumplings can be cut off. Season the mixture with lemon zest, salt,
pepper and nutmeg.
Cut off small dumplings with a teaspoon. Leave pumpkin dumplings in
boiling salted water for approx. 7 minutes.

Roast the onion in a frying pan until lightly fry the tomato cubes, salt
and the chopped parsley.

Arrange pumpkin dumplings in portions with the tomato parsley sauce.
Parmesan to hand.

9.37 Rhubarb cake with sprinkles

Laxative, antipyretic. Protects the digestive system. Detoxifying, affects
anorexia, good to fight flatulence, inflammatory bowel disease, brittle
nails and hair. Relieves pain, detoxifying, against dry skin, acne,
eczema.
Cooking time approx. 1 1/2 hours
Calories p. portion: 476
8 portions
Allergens: AG

Quantity of ingredients:
Wheat flour 7/8 lbs / 400g. (yes)
Cow's milk (whole milk 3.5% fat) 1 cup / 200g. (yes)
Yeast 1 oz / 30g. (yes)
Honey 2 teaspoons / 5g. (yes)
Sunflower oil 2 teaspoons / 5g. (yes)

Lemon peel 1 piece / 3g. (yes)
Salt 1 pinch / 1g. (yes)
Rhubarb 2,2 lbs / 800g. (yes)
Margarine 1/4 lbs - 4oz / 120g. (yes)
Wheat flour 3/4 lbs / 300g. (yes)
Vanilla sugar natural 2 pinches / 1g. (yes)
Cinnamon ground 2 pinches / 1g. (yes)
Honey 5 table spoons / 50g. (yes)

Cooking instructions:
Mix flour, grated lemon peel and salt.
Heat milk gently and mix with yeast and honey.
Then add the flour mixture and the oil and knead vigorously. Cover the dough and let it rise in a warm place until it reaches twice the amount. (about 30 minutes)

For the sprinkles, mix flour with vanilla and cinnamon, then add honey and margarine and crumble to a crumbly mass. Keep the sprinkles dough cool.

Lay out a baking sheet with parchment paper.
Knead the dough for the bottom again, roll it out, place it on the baking sheet and let it rise for another 10 minutes.

Clean the rhubarb, wash it, halve lengthwise and cut into pieces of approx. 3 cm. Spread the pieces on the rolled out dough and crumble the sprinkles over the cake.

Place the cake in the preheated oven at 175 ° C and bake for about 40 minutes.

9.38 Ribbon noodles with leaf spinach

Promotes digestion, improves blood circulation, forcing spleen and intestine, improves pancreatic function, good to fight loss of appetite, flatulence, inflammatory bowel disease, obesity, stomach ulcers, stomach cramps, rheumatism, heartburn, twelffinger intestinal ulcers.
Cooking time approx. 45 min
Calories p. portion: 722
2 portions
Allergens: ACG

Quantity of ingredients:
Spinach 5/8 lbs - 8oz / 250g. (yes)
Salt 1 pinch / 1g. (yes)
Noodles (wheat, ribbon noodles) with egg 5/8 oz / 200g. (yes)
Olive oil 1 table spoon / 15g. (yes)
Onion (spring onion) 1 piece / 20g. (yes)
Cream, sweet 30% 1/2 cup / 100g. (yes)
Créme fraiche cheese 1/2 teaspoon / 6g. (yes)
Thyme dried 1/2 teaspoon / 2g. (yes)
Basil (fresh) 1/2 teaspoon / 2g. (yes)
Oregano dried 1/2 teaspoon / 2g. (yes)
Nutmeg 1 pinch / 0,5g. (yes)
Pepper (ground) 1 pinch / 0,5g. (yes)
Parmesan 1/2 oz / 20g. (yes)
Pine nuts 1 table spoon / 15g. (yes)
Black caraway 1 pinch / 1g. (yes)

Cooking instructions:
Put the dripping wet spinach together with a little salt for 3 minutes in a pot, then drain in a sieve. Then finely cut.

Boil tagliatelle in plenty of salted water.

Heat the oil in a skillet and fry the spring onions rings. Add cream, crème fraiche, thyme, basil, oregano and nutmeg. Stir in the sauce while stirring. Add the spinach, heat briefly, season with nutmeg, salt and pepper.
Drain pasta and mix with the spinach. Season with salt and pepper. Portion noodles and serve with parmesan and pine nuts. Sprinkle the black cumin over it.

9.39 Roasted nuts

Dissolves stones. Good to fight depressions. Strengths spleen and stomach.
Cooking time approx. 5 min
Calories p. portion: 973
2 portions
Allergens: H

Quantity of ingredients:
Hazelnuts 1/4 lbs - 4oz / 100g. (yes)
Cashews 1/4 lbs - 4oz / 100g. (yes)
Walnuts 1/4 lbs - 4oz / 100g. (yes)

Cooking instructions:
Roast nuts in a pan for about 5 minutes.

9.40 Russian kasha with white cabbage

Promotes digestion, relieves pain, detoxifying, promotes digestion,
stimulates appetite, dissolves stagnation, stimulates blood production
and metabolism, reduces fat.
Cooking time approx. 30 min
Calories p. portion: 250
2 portions
Allergens: AG

Quantity of ingredients:
Buckwheat whole grain 1 cup / 130g. (yes)
Water 1 1/2 cups / 240g. (yes)
Nutmeg 1 pinch / 1g. (yes)
Salt 1 pinch / 1g. (yes)
Parsley 1 table spoon / 10g. (yes)
Ground 1 pinch / 2g. (yes)
Butter organic 1 teaspoon / 3g. (yes)
White cabbage Handful / 20g. (yes)

Cooking instructions:
Roast buckwheat golden yellow; add boiling water, heat till it boils
briefly and then let it swell until soft; Grate the white cabbage finely and
fold in. Season with nutmeg, a little salt; some parsley, cumin and butter
at the end.

9.41 Semolina dumpling soup

Reduces blood pressure, strengthens immune system, prevents cancer,
reduces radiation damage, dissolves stagnation, promotes weight loss.
Good to fight immunodeficiency, loss of appetite, flatulence, high blood
pressure, depressions, diabetes, diarrhea.
Cooking time approx. 1 hour
Calories p. portion: 287
3 portions
Allergens: ACGLO

Quantity of ingredients:
Butter organic 1/8 lbs - 2oz / 40g. (yes)
Chicken egg 1 piece / 65g. (little)
Salt 1 pinch / 1g. (yes)
Pepper (ground) 1 pinch / 0,5g. (yes)
Nutmeg 1 pinch / 1g. (yes)
Wheat semolina 3 oz / 80g. (yes)
Basic recipe for a beef soup (warming) 2 cup / 500g. (little)
Parsley 1 table spoon / 10g. (yes)
Chives 1 table spoon / 10g. (yes)

Cooking instructions:
Knead the ingredients for the dumplings to a firm dough and allow to
swell for 30 minutes. Heat the broth (basic recipe for a beef broth
warming). Then cut out with a spoon dumplings, place in the prepared
broth and let stand for 20 minutes. Before serving, chop parsley and
sprinkle with thinly sliced chives.

9.42 Spicy avocado cream with cottage cheese

Anti-inflammatory, good to fight swelling, pain and itching, forcing
spleen and digestive system, detoxifying, bactericide.
Cooking time approx. 15 min
Calories p. portion: 614
4 portions
Allergens: G

Quantity of ingredients:
Avocado 2 pieces / 600g. (yes)
Pepper (ground) 1 pinch / 0,5g. (yes)
Salt 1 pinch / 1g. (yes)
Lemon juice 1/2 piece / 15g. (yes)
Peppers powder 1 pinch / 1g. (yes)
Olive oil 1 table spoon / 10g. (yes)
Herbs various 1 table spoon / 7g. (yes)
Cottage cheese 1 cup / 250g. (recommended)
Bread with carob kernel flour 8 slices / 200g. (yes)

Cooking instructions:
Peel, core and purée avocados; add plenty of ground pepper, salt,
lemon juice, rose paprika, a few drops of oil, chili, fresh chopped herbs,
a pinch of salt; cottage cheese (about the same amount as avocado

cream), carefully submerge.

Goes well with: Potatoes and millet, with which the avocado cream in combination with vegetable dishes, legumes or lettuce leaves a delicious meal. It is also very good as an appetizer, as a souvenir at parties and as a morning meal in the summer together with a mild dish of lentils or Adzuki beans and grated radish.

9.43 Spicy cake with dates

Good to fight loss of appetite, flatulence, inflammatory bowel disease, obesity, gout, stomach ulcers, stomach cramps, rheumatism, heartburn. Calms nerves and stomach, improves blood circulation.
Cooking time approx. 1 1/2 hours
Calories p. portion: 808
4 portions
Allergens: ACGO

Quantity of ingredients:
Sunflower oil 1/2 cup / 100g. (yes)
Sugar white 5/8 oz / 200g. (yes)
Cow's milk (whole milk 3.5% fat) 1/2 cup / 100g. (yes)
Wheat flour 5/8 lbs - 8oz / 250g. (yes)
Cocoa 1/8 lbs - 2oz / 40g. (yes)
Dates dried 1/8 lbs - 2oz / 50g. (yes)
Chicken egg 3 pieces / 180g. (little)
Clove 1/2 teaspoon / 1g. (yes)
Cinnamon ground 1 1/2 tea spoon / 3g. (yes)
Nutmeg 1 pinch / 0,5g. (yes)
Baking powder 1/2 package / 1,5g. (yes)
Butter organic 1 teaspoon / 2g. (yes)
Wheat flour 1 teaspoon / 2g. (yes)

Cooking instructions:
Separate eggs. Stir egg whites until stiff and set aside.
Add oil, sugar, egg yolk to a bowl and stir until frothy.
Add the flour, cocoa and baking powder, stir. Stir in the milk. Now add the minced dates and the spices (the cloves as grated powder) to the mixture and mix with low speed of the hand mixer.
Now, take the stiffly egg white spoonful carefully under.
Put the dough in a greased, floured mold and bake at 200°C/392°F for 70 minutes.

9.44 Summer Salad

Promotes digestion, helps to digest fat, forcing spleen, supports urination, reduces blood pressure. Detoxifying, prevents cancer.
Cooking time approx. 10 min
Calories p. portion: 281
1 portions
Allergens: GMNO

Quantity of ingredients:
Rucola Handful / 15g. (yes)
Radicchio 1 head / 30g. (yes)
Tomato 15 pieces (diced) / 100g. (yes)
Olive oil 1 table spoon / 10g. (yes)
Olives 2 table spoons / 16g. (yes)
Vinegar Aceto Balsamico 1 table spoon / 10g. (yes)
Mustard medium hot 2 teaspoons / 5g. (yes)
Sesame paste (Tahini) 1 teaspoon / 2g. (yes)
Parmesan 2 table spoons / 20g. (yes)
Salt 1 pinch / 0,5g. (yes)
Pepper (ground) 1 pinch / 0,2g. (yes)
Rosemary 2 teaspoons / 3g. (yes)

Cooking instructions:
Wash the salad, pluck it small and arrange it in a bowl.

Sauce: Put the oil, the balsamic vinegar, the mustard and the tahini in a glass with a lid and shake well. Season the dressing with salt and pepper. Mix the salad with the salad dressing and the olives, sprinkle with parmesan and finally with rosemary.

9.45 Sweet potato pancakes with basil pesto

Strengthens the immune system, reduces fat, Improves digestion, calms nerves and stomach, dissolves stones, improves blood circulation, strengthens the muscles, antioxidativ.
Cooking time approx. 30 min
Calories p. portion: 625
3 portions
Allergens: ACH

Quantity of ingredients:
Sweet potato 4 pieces / 500g. (yes)
Onion read 1/2 piece / 30g. (yes)

Basil 1 table spoon / 10g. (yes)
Chicken egg 2 pieces / 140g. (little)
Spelled wholemeal flour 3 oz / 80g. (recommended)
Salt 1 pinch / 0,5g. (yes)
Olive oil 1/4 cup / 20g. (yes)
Salt 1 teaspoon (coarse) / 3g. (yes)
Basil Handful / 15g. (yes)
Parsley Handful / 15g. (yes)
Garlic 2 cloves / 3g. (yes)
Walnuts 1/8 lbs - 2oz / 60g. (yes)
Olive oil 2 table spoons / 20g. (yes)

Cooking instructions:
Sweet Potato Buffer: Wash the sweet potato thoroughly, but do not
peel, and grate into a large bowl. Add onion, basil, egg and flour, mix
well and sprinkle with salt. The mixture can be formed into buffers. Bake
in a preheated tube on a baking tray coated with oil for 4 to 5 minutes
on both sides.

Basil Pesto: Add the salt, chopped basil and parsley and crushed garlic
in a small bowl and crush (if available, use the mortar). Add the grated
walnuts. While stirring, add enough olive oil until the desired
consistency is achieved.

9.46 Tofu-Black Bean Chili with Rice

Supports urination, lowers cholesterol, prevents arteriosclerosis, for the
drainage of the body overweight and high blood pressure, strengthens
immune system.
Cooking time approx. 45 min
Calories p. portion: 344
4 portions
Allergens: AEL

Quantity of ingredients:
Rapeseed oil 1/4 cup / 60g. (yes)
Onion white 2 pieces / 120g. (yes)
Peppers 1 piece / 20g. (yes)
Pepper Cayenne 1 pinch / 0,5g. (yes)
Coriander 1 teaspoon / 2g. (yes)
Thyme 1 teaspoon / 2g. (yes)
Clove 1 teaspoon / 2g. (yes)
Spelled wholemeal flour 2 table spoons / 16g. (recommended)

Sherry (whine) 1 table spoon / 8g. (yes)
Soy Tofu 5/8 lbs - 8oz / 250g. (recommended)
Black beans 2 cans (400g) / 400g. (yes)
Basic recipe for a chicken soup (warming) 1 1/2 cups / 300g. (little)
Bay leaf 1 piece / 0,2g. (yes)
Garlic 6 pieces / 8g. (yes)
Water 6 cups / 400g. (yes)
Rice Basmati 1 cup / 120g. (yes)

Cooking instructions:
Heat the oil at medium temperature in a large saucepan, add onions, paprika and chili powder and fry for 2 minutes until the onions are glassy.
Add the remaining spices, stirring constantly, stirring until the aroma rises.
Dust the flour, fry for 2 minutes and make sure that the paste-like spice mixture does not burn.
Deglaze with sherry, add the black beans (tin) and mix with the spices.
Add the chicken broth, add the bay leaf and stir in the chopped garlic.
Simmer the beans for 30 minutes and add some chicken stock if needed.
Cook the tofu cubes during the last 10 minutes. The tofu can easily disintegrate and should therefore be lifted very gently with a wooden spoon.
Finally, pick out the bay leaf and serve the tofu black bean chili with rice.

9.47 Vanilla cream with berries

Weakness, chronic constipation of the intestine, weight loss, laxative, detoxifying, blood detoxifying. Strengthens the defense. Good to fight fungi infections.
Cooking time approx. 15 min
Calories p. portion: 278
4 portions
Allergens: G

Quantity of ingredients:
Curd cheese 20% 7/8 lbs / 400g. (recommended)
Yogurt (natural, 1.5% fat) 3/8 lbs - 6oz / 150g. (recommended)
Sugar brown 2 teaspoons / 8g. (yes)
Acerola fruit nectar or powder 1 teaspoon / 2g. (yes)
Vanilla sugar natural 3 package / 3g. (yes)

Cream (30% fat) 1/4 lbs - 4oz / 125g. (yes)
Strawberries 1/4 lbs - 4oz / 100g. (yes)
Raspberry 1/4 lbs - 4oz / 100g. (yes)
Blackberry's 1/4 lbs - 4oz / 100g. (yes)
Blueberry 1/4 lbs - 4oz / 100g. (yes)

Cooking instructions:
Mix the curd cheese, yoghurt, sugar, acerola and vanilla sugar with a
hand mixer or whisk until smooth. Beat the whipped cream very stiff,
mix it under the cream. Arrange vanilla cream in portions with the
berries.

9.48 Warming porridge

Strengthens immune system. Diuretic and laxative. Provides vitamin C.
Dissolves stones. Promotes digestion, detoxifying, promotes
perspiration, reduces blood lipids, stimulates, dissolves stagnation.
Cooking time approx. 10 min
Calories p. portion: 357
1 portions
Allergens: AHO

Quantity of ingredients:
Oat flakes (whole grain) 6 table spoons / 60g. (yes)
Fig dried 3 pieces / 15g. (yes)
Star anise 1 piece / 1g. (yes)
Ginger fresh 1 pinch / 0,5g. (yes)
Water 1 cup / 120g. (yes)
Maple syrup 1 table spoon / 10g. (yes)
Walnuts 1 table spoon (chopped) / 8g. (yes)

Cooking instructions:
Soak the dried fruit. Roast Oatmeal dry. Add dried ginger, star anise or
cinnamon, a little grated ginger and boil everything with water to a
mash. With maple syrup sweet. Whip grated walnuts and sprinkle
before serving.

Effect: Suitable for the cold season.
Caution: Fresh ginger does not drink over a long period of time.

9.49 Wild garlic pesto

Improves the flow characteristics of the blood, high vitamin C content, stomach- und blood detoxifying, good to fight arteriosclerosis, high blood pressure.
Cooking time approx. 10 min
Calories p. portion: 796
2 portions
Allergens: G

Quantity of ingredients:
Wild garlic (garlic spinach) 1/4 lbs - 4oz / 125g. (yes)
Parmesan 1 oz / 30g. (yes)
Pine nuts 1/8 lbs - 2oz / 50g. (yes)
Olive oil 1/4 lbs - 4oz / 125g. (yes)
Salt 1 pinch / 1g. (yes)
Pepper (ground) 1 pinch / 0,3g. (yes)

Cooking instructions:
Fresh wild garlic: Wash the wild garlic leaves and dry them carefully. Cut the wild garlic leaves into fine strips.
Dried wild garlic: Leave approx. 80g in 40g of water for 10 minutes.
Carefully roast the pine nuts. The pine nuts should be light brown after roasting. Cut the pine nuts very finely with a large knife or rub them with a nut mill. Pick up some of the seeds to decorate the pesto later.
Place all ingredients in a tall container and chop and mix with a blender. Put the pesto in a bowl or in a glass.
In the fridge, the pesto lasts a while (days to weeks) and is therefore a way to preserve bear's garlic.
You can eat wild garlic pesto as sauce with spaghetti, but it also tastes great with potatoes or bread.

9.50 Yogurt with honey and nuts

Relieves pain, detoxifying, promotes wound healing. Good to fight acute or chronic constipation of the intestine. Dissolves stones.
Cooking time approx. 5 min
Calories p. portion: 258
1 portions
Allergens: GH

Quantity of ingredients:
Yogurt (natural, 3.5% fat) 1/4 lbs - 4oz / 125g. (recommended)
Honey 2 table spoons / 30g. (yes)
Walnuts 1 table spoon / 12g. (yes)

Cooking instructions:
Mix yoghurt with honey and finely chopped nuts.

10 Effects of food

10.1 Use ingredients: recommendable

Adzuki beans
Amaranth
Amaranth Pops
Bitter Herb liqueur
Broad beans (thick beans)
Buckwheat (roasted) Kasha
Bulgur (cereals)
Carob flour, St. john's bread
Chickpeas
Cottage cheese
Cow's milk (1.5% fat)
Cream 10% coffee cream
Curd cheese 20%
Curd cheese 40%
Feta cheese
Fox nut, gorgon nut, makhana
Fresh cheese from soya
Hibiscus
Kidney beans (red)
Kudzu
Mung bean
Oat fusion (baby food)

Pinto beans speckled
Rice (whole grain)
Rice noodles
Sheep's milk yoghurt
Soy flour
Soy Tofu
Soy Tofu smoked
Soya Cuisine (soy cream)
Soybean milk
Soybeans
Soybeans, black
Soybeans, yellow
Spelled (Dark) bread
Spelled flakes
Spelled grain
Spelled semolina
Spelled wholemeal flour
Sunflower seeds
Yoghurt vanilla
Yogurt (natural, 1.5% fat)
Yogurt (natural, 3.5% fat)

10.2 Use ingredients: yes

Acai powder
Acerola fruit nectar or powder
Agar agar (kelp)
Agave nectar
Agrimony
Almond
Almond marzipan
Almond milk
Almond puree
Aloe juice
Angelica root
Anise (Common Fennel)
Apple (sour)
Apple (sweet)

Apple juice (natural cloudy)
Apple puree
Apricot
Apricot dried
Apricot jam
Apricot nectar
Apricots
Apricots juice
Arrowroot
Artichoke
Asparagus (green or white)
Aubergine
Avocado
Baking powder

Balm
Bamboo shoots
Banana
Banana (cooking banana)
Banchatee (green tea)
barberry
Barley
Barley flour
Barley grass powder
Barley grouts
Barley malt
Barley not peeled
Basic recipe for a beef soup
Basic recipe for a duck soup
Basic recipe for a rice soup (Congee)
Basic recipe for a vegetable soup
(nutritious)
Basil
Basil (fresh)
Batavia
Bay leaf
Bean oil
Beans (green, fresh)
Bearberry leaf
Beef bone marrow
Beef meatbones
Beer (alcohol-free)
Beer (alcohol-reduced)
Beer (Pils)
Beer (Top-fermented German dark
beer)
Berries of the season
Berry juice
Bitter Lemon
Bitter liqueur
Bitter orange peel
Black beans
Black caraway
Black fungus mushroom
Black tea
Blackberry dried (unripe fruit)
Blackberry jam
Blackberry leaves
Blackberry´s
Black-eyed peas
Blackthorn (Sloe)
Blue mallow tee
Blueberry
Blueberry dried
Blueberry jam
Blueberry juice
Bocksdorn fruits (Fructus Lycii, Goji,
goji berry dried
Boletus mushroom

Borage
Borage oil
Boxhorn clover seeds
Brazil nuts
Bread roll
Bread with carob kernel flour
Breadcrumbs (wheat bread, bread roll)
Brie cheese
Broccoli
Brown ale
Brussels sprouts
Buckbean
Buckwheat
Buckwheat whole grain
Burdock root tea
Bush beans
Butter beans white
Butter organic
Camembert
Campari
Cantaloupe
Capers in olive oil
Carambola (Star fruit)
Cardamom
Carrot
Carrot (Early Carrot)
Carrot juice without sugar
Cashews
Cauliflower
Celery root
Celery sticks
Cereal coffee
Chamomile
Chamomile tea
Champignon
Channa-Dal
Chanterelle
Chard
Chenpi (chinese tangerine bowl)
Cherry
Cherry (sour)
Cherry compote
Cherry juice
Chervil
Chervil dried
Chestnut puree
Chestnuts
Chicken Blood
Chickweed
Chicory
Chili (pod or ground)
Chinese cabbage
Chinese pearl barley
Chives

Chlorella (fresh water)
Chocolate
Chocolate (Diabetic)
Chrysanthemum blossom tea
Cinnamon ground
Cinnamon sticks
Clarified butter
Clementine
Clementines
Clove
Cocoa
Coconut fat
Coconut flakes
Coconut grated
Coconut meat
Coconut milk
Coffee
Coix (seeds) YiYi Ren
Cola drink
Cola drink (low calorie)
Compote (fruits of the season)
Cooking oil
Coriander
Coriander (fresh)
Corn
Corn (fast polenta)
Corn (roasted)
Corn flour
Corn germ oil
Corn Grease (Polenta)
Corn silk tea
Corn starch
Couscous
Cow's milk (whole milk 3.5% fat)
Cranberries
Cranberry
Cranberry
Cranberry jam
Cranberry juice
Cream (30% fat)
Cream sour 20%
Cream sour 30%
Cream, sweet 30%
Creamer
Créme fraiche cheese
Cress
Crispbread
Cucumber
Cucumber (bitter)
Cucumber (spicy cucumber)
Cumin (Caraway seed)
Curcuma
Currant (black)
Currant (red)

Currant (white)
Currant jam (black)
Currant jam (red)
Currant juice (black)
Currants (black)
Currants (red)
Curry
Curry paste red
Daisy
Dandelion (young plants)
Dandelion juice
Dandelionroots tea
Dashi
Dates dried
Dates red
Deer's Bones
Dill
Dulse (seaweed)
Dyer's broom herb
Edam cheese
Elderberries
Elderberry blossom tee
Emmental cheese
Endive salad
Evening primrose oil
Fennel
Fennel seeds ground
Fennel tea
Fenugreek (Trigonella foenum-graecum)
Fernet Branca (herbal bitter liqueur)
Feta cheese
Fig
Fig dried
Fish sauce
Flower pollen
French beans
Fresh cheese
Fructose (glucose)
Fruit mix juice
Fruit tea
Gail plum
Galangal
Garam Masala powder
Garlic
Gelatin white
Gelee Royal
Gentian root
Gentian root tea
Ginger fresh
Ginger oil
Ginger powder
Ginkgo fruit
Ginseng

Ginseng liqueur
Ginseng root
Goat and sheep's blood
Goat and sheep's brain
Goat and sheep's milk
Goose blood
Goose fat
Gooseberry
Gorgonzola
Gouda cheese
Gourd
Grape juice red
Grape juice white
Grapefruit (Pomelo)
Grapefruit dried peel
Grapefruit juice
Grapes red
Grapes white
Grapeseed oil
Green spelt
Green tea
Greengage
Ground
Ground caraway
Guava
Hawthorn
Hazelnuts
Herbal tea mix
Herbs bitter
Herbs of Provence
Herbs various
Herbs wild
Hibiscus tea
Hijiki
Hokkaido pumpkin
Honey
Honey wine (Met)
Hop
Horehound leaves
Hyssop
Iceberg lettuce
Jasmine blossoms tee
Juniper berry
Kaki plum
Kalmus
King Solomon's-seal
Kiwi
Kohlrabi
Kombu seaweed (Saccharina japonica)
Kukicha tea
Kumquats
Ladyfingers
Lamb bones
Lamb's lettuce

Lamb's lettuce
Lavender blossoms
Leaf salads (bitter)
Leek
Lemon
Lemon Balm (dried)
Lemon Balm (fresh)
Lemon juice
Lemon peel
Lemongrass
Lentils
Lentils black
Lentils red
Lentils yellow
Lettuce
Licorice root tea
Lily bulbs
Lima beans
Lime
Lime blossom tea
Linseed
Linseed (crushed)
Linseed oil
Liver smoothing tea
Longane
Loquate / Japanese medlar
Lotus roots
Lotus seeds
Lovage
Lovage seeds
Luo Han Guo fruit
Lychee
Lychee in Preserved
Lychee liqueur
Lye roll
Mallow (Malva sylvestris) blossom tea
Malt
Mango
Mango juice
Manioc flour
Maple syrup
Margarine
Margarine (diet)
Marjoram
Martini
Mascarpone cheese
Mayonnaise 50%
Mayonnaise 80%
Medlar
Millet
Millet flakes
Mineral water
Mirabelle plum
Miso

Miso black (fermented)
Miso paste (soy bean paste)
Mixed Pickles
Mold cheese
Morel (black, dried)
Morel, dried
Mu Erh Mushroom
Muesli
Mulberry fruit
Mulled Wine Spice
Multi-grain bread (gray bread)
Mung bean sprouting
Mustard
Mustard Dijon
Mustard medium hot
Mustard seeds
Mustard sweet
Nasturtium (nose-twister or nose-tweaker)
Nectarine
Nettles
Noodles (wheat) with egg
Noodles (wheat, lasagne) with egg
Noodles (wheat, ribbon noodles) with egg
Noodles (wheat, spaghetti) with egg
Nori, purple seaweed, red algae
Nutmeg
Oat
Oat flakes (whole grain)
Oat flakes roasted
Oat flour
Oat meal
Oat milk
Okra
Olive oil
Olives
Olives green
Onion (shallot)
Onion (spring onion)
Onion read
Onion white
Orange
Orange blossom
Orange dried peel
Orange grated peel
Orange jam
Orange juice
Orange peel
Oregano dried
Oregano fresh
Oyster mushroom
Oyster shell powder
Palm oil

Papaya
Parmesan
Parsley
Parsley root
Parsnip
Passion blossoms tea
Passion fruit
Peaches
Peaches (canned)
Peanut (roasted)
Peanut butter
Peanut oil
Peanuts
Pear
Pear juice
Pearl barley
Pearl barley
Peas
Peas, green
Pepper (ground)
Pepper Cayenne
Pepper powder (hot)
Pepper white (ground)
Peppercorns
Peppermint
Peppermint tea
Pepperoni
Pepperoni, red, pitted, halved
Pepperoni, yellow, pitted, halved
Peppers
Peppers (rose peppers)
Peppers (sweet)
Peppers powder
Pickle
Pig blood
Pigeon egg
Pimento
Pine nuts
Pineapple
Pineapple (from a can)
Pineapple juice without sugar
Pistachios
Plum
Plum dried
Plums
Pomegranate
Poppy
Pork brain
Pork Lard
Pork lung
Pork marrow bones
Pork skin
Pork's intestine
Potato

Potato (mealy)
Potato flour
Prickly pear
Processed cheese 12%
processed cheese 30%
Prosecco
Psyllium seed
Pudding powder vanilla
Puff pastry
Pumpernickel (dark bread)
Pumpkin
Pumpkin seed oil
Pumpkin seeds
Quince
Quinoa
Radicchio
Radish
Radish (white, green, purple-red)
Radish black
Radish horseradish
Radish leaves
Raisins
Rapeseed oil
Raspberry
Raspberry dried (immature)
Raspberry jam
Raspberry leaf tea
Red beet
Red berry (without sugar)
Red cabbage
Red wine
Reishi mushroom
Rhubarb
Ribworttea
Rice (fragrance)
Rice (Gaoliang / Sorghum)
Rice Basmati
Rice black
Rice flour
Rice long grain rice
Rice malt
Rice mash
Rice red
Rice round grain
Rice starch
Rice sticky
Rice sweet
Rice variety any
Rice wild (nature rice)
Romaine lettuce / lettuce salad
Rose blossom tea
Rose hip
Rose hip tea
Rose leaf tea

Rosemary
Rucola
Rum
Rusk
Rye
Rye flour
Rye wholemeal bread
Safflower (Dyer's thistle / Hong Hua)
Saffron
Sage
Sago (cereals)
Sake
Salsify
Salt
Salt (herbal)
Sauerkraut (cutted cabbage fermented)
Savory
Savoy cabbage / kale
Sea buckthorn
Sesame oil
Sesame oil roasted
Sesame paste (Tahini)
Sesame, black
Sesame, white
Sheep's milk
Sherry (whine)
Shiitake, dried
Sorrel
Sour cherries
Sour milk cheese 20%
Sourdough
Soy noodles
Soy sauce
Soybean oil
Soybeans, blacks, fermented
Spinach
Spirit
St. Benedict's thistle, blessed thistle,
holy thistle, spotted thistle
Star anise
Stevia (candyleaf, sweetleaf)
Strawberries
Strawberry jam
Strawberry Juice
Sugar - icing sugar
Sugar brown
Sugar candy white
Sugar cane sugar
Sugar fructose - fruit sugar
Sugar glucose - grapes sugar
Sugar Milk Sugar
Sugar molasses
Sugar palm sugar
Sugar substitute (sweetener)

Sugar white
Sunflower oil
Sweet potato
Tabasco
Tangerine
Tarragon (Estragon)
Tea mixture uric acid lowering
Thistle oil
Thyme
Thyme dried
Toast bread (whole grain)
Tomato
Tomato dried
Tomato juice
Tomato paste
Tomato puree
Tonic Water
Topinambur
Truffle
Tsampa (roasted barley flour)
Turmeric (yellow root)
Turnip
Turnips
Umeboshi paste
Umeboshi plums (Japanese apricots)
Valerian
Vanilla
Vanilla pod
Vanilla powder
Vanilla sugar natural
Vegetable juice
Vinegar (Apple vinegar)
Vinegar (Red wine vinegar)
Vinegar Aceto Balsamico
Vinegar Aceto Balsamico white
Wakame
Walnut oil
Walnuts
Walnuts roasted
Water
Water hot

Watermelon
Wax gourd
Wheat
Wheat beer
Wheat bran
Wheat bulgur
Wheat flakes
Wheat flatbread/pita bread
Wheat flour
Wheat flour whole grain
Wheat germ oil
Wheat semolina
Wheat semolina for children
Wheat/Rye/Gray-black bread with yeast
Wheatgrass juice
Wheatgrass powder
Whey
White beans
White bread (baguette)
White bread (pretzel sticks)
White bread (roll)
White bread (wheat bread)
White breadcrumbs
White cabbage
White dumpling bread (wheat bread cut into chunks)
White wine
Whole grain bread
Wholemeal flour
Wild garlic (garlic spinach)
Wild herbs
Wild strawberries
Wormwood
Wormwood herb
Yam root, yam root tuber
Yarrow
Yarrow tea
Yeast
Yew nut
Yogi tea
Zucchini

10.3 Use ingredients: little

Basic recipe for a beef soup (warming)
Basic recipe for a chicken soup (warming)
Basic recipe for a fish soup
Beef soup meat
Butter (half fat)
Buttermilk
Caviar
Chicken egg

Chicken egg white
Chicken meat
Chicken yolk
Codfish
Cream sour 10%
Flounder
Freshwater fish
Halibut (Flatfish)
Kefir

Mare's milk
Mediterranean fish (cod, plaice, haddock, sea eel, mackerel)
Noodles (whole grain) with egg
Perch
Plaice

Quail egg
Skim milk powder
Sour cream 15% fat
Sour milk
Whitefish

10.4 Do not use contra-acting foods

Anchovy / Sardine
Beef fillet
Beef heart
Beef heart (calf)
Beef kidney
Beef liver
Beef lungs (calf)
Beef meat
Beef meat (calf)
Beef Oxtail pieces
Beef stomach
Calamari
Carp
Chicken heart
Chicken liver
Chicken stomach
Cod
Crab
Crucian
Deer meat
Deer meat
Deer's kidneys
Duck (heart)
Duck (slaughtered)
Ducks egg
Eel
Eel smoked
Fish innards
Fish pieces mixed (fresh water)
Fish remains
Fresh cheese with herbs
Freshwater crab
Goat
Goat and sheep's liver
Goat and sheep's stomach
Goat cheese
Goose
Goose egg
Goose parts
Grass carp
Herring
Horse meat
Jellyfish
Lamb kidneys
Lamb liver

Lamb meat
Lamb shoulder
Lobster
Mackerel
Mozzarella
Mullet
Mussels
Mutton
Mutton
Octopus
Octopus
Oysters
Pheasant
Pigeon
Pork Bacon
Pork fat (lard)
Pork ham
Pork ham cooked
Pork ham smoked
Pork heart
Pork kidneys
Pork knuckle
Pork liver
Pork meat
Pork sausage (Bratwurst)
Pork stomach
Pork/beef sausage (smoked)
Quail
Rabbit
Rabbit (wild)
Rabbit liver
Rabbit meat
Rosefish
Salmon
Sea cucumber
Seacrab
Shark
Shrimp
Shrimps
Slug
Spiny lobsters
Spurdog (spiny dogfish, Schillerlocken)
Supplementary nutrition
Trout
Trout (smoked)

Tuna   Turkey ham
Turkey breast meat   Wild boar meat

11 Herbs and their effects

11.1 Basil

It has a beneficial effect on flatulence and nausea, relaxing and soothing. Good to fight emphysema, bronchitis, whooping cough, high blood pressure, headache, mouth odor, warts, hiccup, gout, migraine.

11.2 Nettles

Promotes urination. Tea or juice, cleanses the blood and the kidneys, supports prostate problems, inhibit the formation of inflammation, pain-relieving.

11.3 Dill

The medicinal and spice herb has an antispasmodic effect and stimulates gastric juice production. Good to fight flatulence. Antispasmodic for gastrointestinal discomfort.

11.4 Chervil dried

Forces urination, detoxifying, blood-purifying and blood-pressure-reducing effects.

11.5 Coriander

The essential oils are appetizing, digestive, cramping and soothing in stomach and intestinal disorders.

11.6 Herbs various

Appetizing, lots of trace elements and vitamins

11.7 Chives

Bactericide, prevents cancer, strengthens gastric juice production, promotes digestion and blood circulation, promotes growth, triggers stagnation.

11.8 Lovage

Stimulates digestion, reduces pain. Extracts of the root are used to flush out urinary tract infections and prevent kidney gravel.

11.9 Dandelion (young plants)

Detoxifies, relieves inflammation. Regulates digestion, helps with rheumatism, releases kidney stones, leaves pimples and chronic skin disorders disappear.

11.10 Marjoram

Helps to digest fat foods, strengthens digestive organs, helps to fight colds, strengthens menstruation, promotes skin healing.

11.11 Oregano dried

It has an anti-digestive, calming and nerve-strengthening effect, helps to fight cramping stomach and intestinal disorders. The ingredient Carvacrol has an anti-inflammatory effect.

11.12 Parsley

Stimulates liver function, detoxifies. Forces urinating. Relieves flatulence. Digestive and menstrual stimulating, birth-accelerating, memory-enhancing, blood-purifying, skin-smoothing.

11.13 Peppermint

Relaxes, frees the lungs and the nose (inhale), regulates the cycle. Stimulates bile flow and bile production, antispasmodic in gastrointestinal disorders, antimicrobial and antiviral.

11.14 Rosemary

Promotes digestion, relieves bloating, strengthens lung, spleen and kidney. Affects the circulation and nerves. Appetizing. Baths help to fight circulatory disorders as well as with gout and rheumatism.

11.15 Black caraway

Detoxifying, immunoregulatory. In addition, the oil should stimulate the formation of bone marrow cells and generally protect body cells from viruses.

11.16   Thyme dried

Disinfecting. It stimulates the blood circulation, increases the appetite and helps to digest fat meat better. Strengthens lungs and spleen (TCM).

12 Basics of Nutrition

The basic principles of nutrition described herein are general recommendations. They are not aimed at a specific form of therapy. Recommendations concerning a therapy have priority.

12.1 Nutrition

Regular meals in a relaxed atmosphere. A warm breakfast is considered a good start into the day.
The main meals ought to be taken for lunch – supper in the early evening. Pay attention to feeling hungry or sated: don't eat too much nor remain hungry is the rule
Prepare the meals freshly from natural, regional products. Frozen, heat-conserved, industrially prepared or foodstuffs cooked in the microwave oven are rejected.
Choice of foodstuffs according to the season: more cooling food in summer, more warming food in winter.
Eat cooked food at least twice a day. Food and drinks ought to be lukewarm, never ice-cold or hot.
Raw vegetables, briefly cooked vegetables, freshly squeezed juices and mineral water are not recommended. Milk and dairy products are only included in the diet if they don't cause problems.
Don't use therapeutic recipes over a longer period without consulting your doctor or therapist.

Varied food
Enjoy the diversity of foodstuffs. Characteristics of a balanced nutrition are variety, suitable combination and a balanced quantity of rich and low energy foodstuffs (on one hand avoiding undersupply with essential nutrients and on the other hand to take to many undesirable substances).

A lot of Cereal Products - and Potatoes
Bread, pasta, rice, cereal flakes (best wholemeal) as well as potatoes contain almost no fat, but many vitamins, mineral nutrients, trace elements, roughage and secondary plant substances. These foodstuffs ought to be taken with low-fat side dishes.

Vegetables and Fruit – „Take Five" every day ...
5 portions of vegetables and fruit a day, as fresh as possible, briefly cooked, or maybe one portion as a juice – ideal as a side dish to every meal as well as snack between meals: Thus a lot of vitamins, mineral nutrients as well as roughage and secondary plant substances

Daily milk and dairy products
Milk and Dairy Products every Day, once or twice per Week Fish; meat, sausages as well as eggs moderately. These foodstuffs contain valuable nutrients like calcium in the milk, iodine selenium and omega-3 fat acids in saltwater fish. Meat is favorable due to its high content of disposable iron and the vitamins B1, B6 and B12. Quantities of 300 – 600 g meat and sausage per week are sufficient. Prefer low-fat products, especially in meat- and dairy products.

Low-fat and fatty Foodstuffs
Fat supplies us with essential fat acids and fatty foodstuffs contain also fat-soluble vitamins. Fat is high in energy; therefore much fat in the food may cause overweight, possibly also cancer. Too many saturated fat acids may further a tendency for cardio-vascular diseases in the long term. Prefer vegetable oils and fats (e.g. rapeseed-, olive-, soya-oils and solid fats produced therefrom). Beware of invisible fat in meat- and dairy products, pastry and sweets as well as in fast-food and convenience foods. 70 – 90 g fat per day is sufficient.

Moderately Sugar and Salt
Take sugar and foods/drinks containing various kinds of sugar (e.g. glucose syrup) only occasionally. Use herbs and spices as well as a little salt creatively. Prefer salt containing iodine.

Plenty of Liquids
Water is absolutely essential. Drink 1-2 l liquids every day. Prefer water (with or without gas) and other low-calorie drinks. Alcoholic drinks should not be taken.

Tasty Dishes, carefully cooked
Cook the meals with as low temperatures and as short as possible, using little water and fat – this preserves the original taste, keeps the nutrients intact and prevents the production of harmful compounds.

Take time and enjoy the food
Take your Time and enjoy your Food
Eating consciously helps to eat right. The eye enjoys food, too. It's fun, invites to enjoy varied dishes and stimulates the feeling of satiety.

Watch your Weight and stay in Motion
A balanced diet and a lot of exercise and sport (30 – 60 min/day) are a healthy combination. The right weight furthers well-being and health. Thermals, directional effectiveness, digestive power

There are various criteria for judging the effectiveness of herbs and foodstuffs.

The use of certain herbs and ingredients is based on observations of the effects on the body which these foodstuffs, herbs and spices show after having eaten them. The medical science has developed following system: Every ingredient or herb has a directional effectiveness. Furthermore, there are herbs which have a special effect on certain organs.

The basic condition for a healthy metabolism is to obtain sufficient energy from food and that the digestive process doesn't use too much energy.

An easily digestible meal makes content and sated, doesn't cause flatulence and fatigue after the meal. The perfect spices increase the healthiness of our meals. Very often, just small doses of herbs and spices will suffice. They are not used to make us sated, but to help our digestive organs to digest the food.

12.2 Recipes

The recipes list the ingredients to be used and the cooking instructions show how the dish is prepared. The list of ingredients shows the concerned quantities as well as the relevance for the therapy. If you find „less than mentioned", try to comply or find an alternative from the „list of recommended foodstuffs". Mostly it shall result just in a small change of taste when you simply avoid this ingredient.

Mild cooking methods: boiling, stewing, poaching, steaming
Strong cooking methods: barbecuing, roasting, frying, smoking
Balanced cooking methods: deep-frying, baking brick
Deep-freezing and warming in the microwave oven should be avoided (denaturalization).

12.3 Foodstuffs

Foodstuffs have an effect on body and soul like medicinal herbs, only a very much milder one. Dietary advice is mainly based on regional foodstuffs. The knowledge about the effects of each foodstuff and the knowledge, when which foodstuff shall be used, is based on the orthodoschool of medicine. Use ecologic-organic products, if possible. As everything should be cooked for a long time due to a better digestability and very rarely eaten raw, the food agrees with everyone.

The classification of the foodstuffs according to their effect on the body is the basis in order to achieve a harmonious status of health.

Dietary advisors do not recommend certain foodstuffs for everyone. The individual diet is tailor-made for the individual constitution.

Buy only fresh and ripe fruit and vegetables. You ought to leave unripe fruit and vegetables and such with brown spots and wilted leaves behind in the market. In this case take deep-frozen goods (never ready-to-serve dishes!). Fruit and vegetables are deep-frozen immediately after harvesting and often contain more vitamins and minerals than the goods from the vegetable shelf. Whereas conserved or tinned goods contain very much less biological substances. Also, salt, sugar and others are mostly added to the latter. Never leave the foodstuffs in the water after washing them to avoid that many vital substances get drowned. Clean salads, fruit and vegetables immediately before serving.

Please make sure of the hygienic processing of foodstuffs. Clean your salads, fruit and vegetables carefully. When cooking with meat, prepare all ingredients first and then process the meat products. Clean the worktop and tools very carefully. Wooden surfaces ought to be treated with a mild disinfectant regularly in order to reduce germination.

Store fruit and vegetables separately, if possible. Harvested fruit and vegetables are still alive and emit e.g. ethylene gas, which makes other products ripen and age faster. Keep meat and fish in the closed packaging or store them in the fridge in closed containers.

12.4 Herbs

There are some basic rules for storing medicinal herbs. On principle, herbs must be protected from direct sunlight, humidity and heat.

Containers for the storage of herbs may be glasses, ceramic jars and even plastic containers. However, plastic is a rather unsuitable material and should only be a short-term solution. In case of glass containers, use a dark material.

Medicinal herbs cannot be kept for any long period. The shelf life of herbs is limited. However, it can be prolonged with suitable storage. The place should be dark, rather cool and absolutely dry. A wooden medicine cabinet, placed not directly next to a source of heat, would be ideal. Never buy large quantities of herbs so as not to have to throw them away. Label the container with the name of the herb and the date of harvesting or processing.

13 Other dietic-books

The following syndromes of dietetics, TCM or for a therapy supplement for cancer are available.

Dietetics

E001. Nutrition of the infant - baby food
E002. Nutrition during lactation
E003. Nutrition in old age
E004. Nutrition of children and adolescents
E005. Nutrition of athletes
E006. Light weight
E007. Pregnancy
E008. Full food

Protein and electrolyte - kidneys
E009. (hemodialysis) dialysis treatment
E010. Acute renal failure
E011. Chronic renal insufficiency
E012. Nephrotic syndrome
E013. Kidney stones (nephrolithiasis)

Gastrointestinal tract - pancreas
E014. Acute pancreatitis (inflammation of the pancreas)
E015. Chronic pancreatitis (inflammation of the pancreas)

Gastrointestinal tract - small intestine and large intestine
E016. Acute obstipation (constipation)
E017. Chronic obstipation (constipation)
E018. Colon irritabile
E019. Diverticulitis
E020. Acquired lactose intolerance (lactose malabsorption)
E021. Fructose malabsorption
E022. Glutensensitive enteropathy (celiac disease)
E023. Colectomy
E024. Short Bowel Syndrome

Gastrointestinal tract - liver, gallbladder, bile ducts
E025. Acute and chronic hepatitis (inflammation of the liver)
E026. Cholelithiasis (bile stones)
E027. fatty liver
E028. cirrhosis

Gastrointestinal tract - Stomach and duodenal intestine
E029. Acute gastritis
E030. Chronic gastritis
E031. Stomach bleeding
E032. Ulcus ventriculi and duodenal ulcer
E033. Condition after gastric surgery

Gastrointestinal tract - oral cavity and esophagus
E034. Stomatitis
E035. Esophageal carcinoma (esophageal cancer)
E036. Refluosophagitis (heartburn)

Special diseases
E037. Phenylketonuria (PKU)
E038. Rheumatic joint diseases

Metabolism
E039. Obesity (overweight)
E040. Diabetes mellitus
E041. Eating disorders (underweight)

Fat metabolism
E042. Hypercholesterolaemia (increased cholesterol level)
E043. Hepatic Encephalopathy

Heart and circulation
E044. Arteriosclerosis (arterial calcification)
E045. Heart insufficiency
E046. Hypertension
E047. Hyperuricaemia and gout

Changed nutrient requirements
E048. In case of fever
E049. For malignant diseases
E050. After burns
E051. Radiation and chemotherapy

CANCER
E100. Pancreatic cancer
E101. Bladder cancer
E102. Blood cancer (leukemia)
E103. Breast cancer
E104. Colorectal cancer
E105. Gastric cancer
E106. Kidney cancer
E107. Esophageal cancer

TCM
E200. Bladder - moisture heat in the bladder
E201. Bladder - moisture and cold in the bladder
E202. Bladder - emptiness and cold in the bladder
E203. Large intestine - external cold affects the large intestine
E204. Large intestine - moisture heat in the large intestine
E205. Large intestine - heat blocks the intestine II acute
E206. Large intestine - dryness of the colon
E207. Large intestine - Yang deficiency (cold)
E208. Heart - Blood insufficiency
E209. Heart - Blood stagnation
E210. Heart - Fire
E211. Heart - Hot mucus clogs the heart pores

E212. Heart - Cold mucus clogs the heart pores
E213. Heart - Qi deficiency
E214. Heart - Yang deficiency
E215. Heart - Yin deficiency
E216. Liver - Ascending Liver Yang
E217. Liver - Blood deficiency
E218. Liver - Blood stagnation
E219. Liver - Moisture heat in liver and gall bladder
E220. Liver - Fire
E221. Liver - Gall bladder Qi-Empty
E222. Liver - Cold in the liver meridian
E223. Liver - Qi stagnation
E224. Liver - Wind
E225. Liver - Wind with ascending liver Yang
E226. Liver - Wind with blood anemic
E227. Liver - Wind with extreme heat
E228. Lung - Qi deficiency
E229. Lung - Mucus-moisture in the lungs
E230. Lung - Mucus-heat in the lungs
E231. Lung - Mucus-cold in the lungs
E232. Lung - Dryness of the lungs
E233. Lung - Wind-heat attacks the lungs
E234. Lung - Wind-cold affects the lungs
E235. Lung - Yin deficiency
E236. Stomach - Bloodstagnation
E237. Stomach - Fire
E238. Stomach - Cold with liquid
E239. Stomach - Nutrition stagnation
E240. Stomach - Qi deficiency
E241. Stomach - Rebellious Qi
E242. Stomach - Yin Emptiness
E243. Spleen - Heat and moisture attack the spleen
E244. Spleen - Coldness and moisture affects the spleen
E245. Spleen - Qi deficiency
E246. Spleen - Qi deficiency + Declining spleen Qi
E247. Spleen - Qi deficiency + spleen does not control the blood
E248. Spleen - Yang deficiency
E249. Kidney - Heart and kidney no longer communicate
E250. Kidney - Jing deficiency
E251. Kidney - Kidneys cannot receive the Qi
E252. Kidney - Qi is not stable
E253. Kidney - Yang deficiency
E254. Kidney - Yin deficiency

For further information visit di-book.com.